Bigfoot Untold

Story by Supriati Sample
Written by Ricko Dupri Sample

Bigfoot Untold
Copyright © 2018 by Ricko Dupri Sample

All rights reserved. No part of this publication may be reproduced, distributed, or transmitted in any form or by any means, including photocopying, recording, or other electronic or mechanical methods, without the prior written permission of the author, except in the case of brief quotations embodied in critical reviews and certain other non-commercial uses permitted by copyright law.

Tellwell Talent
www.tellwell.ca

ISBN
978-0-2288-0678-3 (Paperback)

About the Author

At fourteen, Ricko Sample is currently in his second year of college. He works as a model and actor and lives with his family in Auburn, Washington. *Bigfoot Untold* is his first book.

About the Book

In 2008, five-year-old Alice Adkins goes missing near her home in rural Crowded Lake, Washington. When she returns, she has a story about a big monster that is raising concerns over a local menace believed to be Bigfoot. And though everything is not as it seems, over the next nine years, Alice and her family will have other encounters that make it clear there is something out there in the wilds of Washington State.

Table of Contents

Chapter I
Where's Alice? 1

Chapter II
"Something doesn't appear right…" 9

Chapter III
Unwanted Ingredient 15

Chapter IV
Early Arrival 20

Chapter V
Reveals & Fireflies 25

Chapter VI
Visiting a Sick Relative 32

Chapter VII
"Someone must have been very hungry." 38

Chapter VIII
Destruction & Relocation 43

Afterword 49

Chapter I
Where's Alice?

In the town of Crowded Lake, Washington, everybody knew each other. It only had a population of around 1,500, and everybody treated each other like a family. The town was split into three areas. There was one large area that was cut off from the rest of the town by a river that flowed from the lake, and the two smaller areas that were split by big farms on the more rural side of the river. Most houses had big gardens, which were usually surrounded by farms. Everybody in the neighborhood worked hard. Some worked in the city far away, and others worked close by, farming, fishing, or pursuing other trades and ventures. The nearest city from Crowded Lake was around twenty miles away. The town was divided by a river, with one side consisting of more gardens, shrubs, trees, and fewer houses. Most of the houses were made of wood.

The Adkins family was one of many that had a lot of history connected to the town of Crowded Lake. They lived near the river by the bridge. Due to this family's long history living there, some of their relatives knew of the existence of an abnormal creature living around the town. And they weren't the only ones. Across the street, there were a few houses with big gardens surrounding them connected to a giant farm.

It was a late afternoon in the summer of 2008, and five-year-old Alice Adkins was playing outside in a nearby playground in front of her house. She was wearing her favorite yellow sleeveless dress—along with her red sandals with a yellow flower design on top of it. Her hair was wavy, like her father's, but also long. Her mother liked to put her hair in a ponytail. Alice was very playful and friendly to her friends; however, she was also very adventurous and never wanted to stay home.

On this particular afternoon, she was playing with a bunch of friends, some of whom were older than her. Some were playing hopscotch, others were playing tag. Alice started to wander away from her friends and was visibly exhausted. She had been playing for about an hour and a half.

"Hey," she said, "I'm going to sit down now."

Josie, one of her friends, came up to her. "Okay, I have to go home anyway. Bye Alice!"

"Okay, see you later!" Alice said.

Alice sat down by herself on a bench. She watched the other kids play in the park. The other kids were having fun hanging out with each other during the hot summer afternoon.

In the Adkins house, Alice's mother and grandmother, Kayla and Mara, were preparing for dinner. Mara Ayala was old but feisty and brave. Kayla was smart and also feisty, but she did get scared a bit easily. They both had long and curly hair, but they usually tied their hair up. Ronald Adkins, Alice's father, was on the phone. He was the most laid-back member of the household. He was also brave and tall, but he didn't talk a lot. His hair was wavy and short. Alice's nine-year-old brother, Alex, was playing video games. Alex was smart and tall like his father. His hair was curly, like his mother's. However, he usually had his hair cut to be shorter. Their house was located between two other houses in the town. On the right, next to a neighbor's house, there was a river, and on the left, next to the other house, there was a big garden.

"Hey everyone," called Kayla, "Dinner time!"

Everybody started walking to their chairs. Kayla and Mara had cooked mash potatoes, barbecued chicken, biscuits, and asparagus. Most of the family enjoyed dinner time, as Kayla and Mara were always cooking something special. Kayla then realized that Alice was not around.

"Where's Alice?" she asked.

Mara also did not know where Alice was. "I have not seen Alice since five! I thought she would be back home by now."

"She was playing outside with her friends," said Alex jumping into the conversation.

Kayla was a bit worried. "Why isn't she home by now?"

She got up from the table and walked to the front window of the house.

"Maybe she's still playing outside," Alex said.

Kayla approached a window and looked outside. Nobody was around. It was dinner time, and everybody was back at their houses.

"Everybody is gone," Kayla said. "I don't see anyone."

Mara then gave a reasonable explanation. "Oh, maybe she just went to visit one of her close friends' houses."

Kayla decided to look for her because it was getting late, and she was very worried. She went outside and headed to her neighbor Annabelle's house. Kayla knocked on the door. A few seconds later, the door cracked open. Annabelle had been having dinner.

"Hello Kayla!" she said. "What can I do for you? You seem a bit frantic, can I get you something to drink? Come on in."

It's true Kayla was frantic.

"No, I can't come in right now. I'm looking for Alice. Have you seen her? She was playing outside with her friends, and Josie might have been with her."

Annabelle saw that Kayla was very concerned about Alice.

"No, unfortunately I haven't seen her. I'll ask Josie, just wait a second."

She went back inside the house. Audible chatter could be heard from Kayla's position as Annabelle spoke to her daughter. A few seconds later, she appeared at the door again.

"Josie says she was hanging out with her, but she doesn't know where she went. She came home early while Alice was still outside. Oh dear, I hope you find her!"

Disappointed, Kayla said, "Well, thank you for trying. I'm sorry for bothering you."

"Oh, it's no problem at all!" Annabelle said, feeling pity for Kayla. "I wish I could help. I will look out for her."

"Thank you, Annabelle. I appreciate it."

Kayla then headed off to the other neighbors.

About an hour later, Kayla returned to the house, tired and exhausted.

She sighed and said, "I have been searching all over the neighborhood, and nobody knows where she has gone!"

Ronald then proposed an explanation. "It is possible that Bigfoot could be involved with this."

Kayla disregarded this. "Don't be so ridiculous, Ronald. I don't think Bigfoot took Alice."

"Well," he said, "there are cases where there was a possibility that Bigfoot was behind the disappearance."

All of them start getting worried for Alice. Suddenly, there was a knock on the door. After the knock, there was a calling from outside. It was Alice's voice.

"Mommy, mommy! Open the door, it's Alice!"

Kayla rushed to the door and opened it. Kayla started crying and hugged her daughter.

"Alice, we've been searching everywhere for you!" Kayla said. "Where have you been!?"

"Hey everyone!" said Alex excitedly from the living room. "Alice is back!"

"Oh, I'm so happy you're home and okay!" Ronald said.

Mara gave a sigh of relief. "Thank God that my beautiful grandchild is home and safe with us."

"Are you hungry, sweetie?" Kayla asked. "Do you want something to eat?"

"No, I'm good." Alice said. "I just want some cookies."

They went to the living room, and Alice sat down on the couch while Kayla went to the kitchen to bring some cookies.

When Kayla came back, she sat by Alice and spoke softly to her.

"Sweetie, where have you been? Tell me what happened."

"I was taken by a big monster!" said Alice.

"A big monster?" Kayla sounded uncertain.

"It looked like the creature that grandma talks about," said Alice. "Bigfoot!"

In a house nearby, a female figure was standing in front of a window. She stared at Alice and Kayla talking to each other through the windows. This female figure soon walked away into a room of the house.

Chapter II

"Something doesn't appear right..."

Kayla continued questioning Alice, still confused.

"Are you sure, sweetie?" she asked. "It could have been a criminal in a disguise. I can call the police right now to make sure."

Mara entered the room after overhearing the conversation.

"Kayla, I think Alice is telling the truth. Remember, there was an unfortunate event that happened to your niece when she was five months old. She was kidnapped by Bigfoot, as well."

About four years previous, relatives of the Adkins family, the Duncan family, were victim to an incident. It was early evening. The house was not in Crowded Lake but about thirty minutes away. The nearest city from there was around thirty miles away. There were large trees and bushes that connected to a giant farm across the street from the Duncans' house. The houses usually were far apart, and the town had lots of space. The houses normally had large households. The Duncan family, however, was small. The house itself was small. It was made out of wood and was surrounded by shrubbery and gardens. In front of their house, there were a few groups of houses.

Isabelle Duncan, the daughter of the Duncan family, was five months old. Sandra Duncan, the mother, was in Isabelle's room, putting Isabelle in her crib. Sandra was playing with her baby while she was in the crib to get her to fall asleep. Then, Isabelle started crying. Sandra tried to calm her down.

"I know, I know," Sandra said. "You're tired and hungry. Shhhh, you can have some milk now."

Sandra gave Isabelle a milk bottle, and the baby stopped crying, and soon fell asleep. Sandra went to the kitchen to cook dinner for her husband.

After Sandra left the room, Bigfoot entered through a window. He took the baby out of the crib and went back out of the window.

A few minutes later, Thomas Duncan, the father of Isabelle, arrived home. Before he entered the driveway, he saw something moving in the backyard. He disregarded it as his imagination playing tricks on him; however, he was still concerned about his daughter. He entered through the front door with his key.

"Honey," he called out excitedly, "I'm home! Where are you?"

"I'm in the kitchen, Thomas!"

"Oh, here you are!" Thomas said. "What are you cooking for dinner?"

"It's your favorite food," she said. "Why don't you change your clothes and get cleaned up while I prepare dinner?"

Thomas started getting undressed and then asked, "Where's Isabelle?"

"She's in her crib, asleep," Sandra said.

"I'll go check on her."

Thomas went to Isabelle's room. It was dark, and the lights were off. Thomas turned on the lights and was shocked, because he couldn't see Isabelle in her crib.

"Sandra!" he yelled, "Where's Isabelle? She's not in her crib! Where did you put her?"

Sandra rushed towards the room. "She's supposed to be in her crib. What are you talking about?"

"She is not here," he said. "The crib is empty!"

"Oh no! Where is my baby? She was here, asleep! I had to cook because I knew you were going to be hungry when you got home!"

Thomas starts thinking. "She must have crawled out."

"That's impossible," she said. "The crib is too tall for her!"

Thomas started searching around. He noticed that the window is slightly open, which he did not see when he first entered the room.

"Look! The window has been opened. Somebody was here. The kidnapper might have escaped through the window."

With this knowledge, Sandra and Thomas started searching more. They exited their house and quickly started moving around outside and asking for help. Thomas called the police. Sandra went to a nearby neighbor's house to ask if they'd seen someone take Isabelle. She knocked on the door and the neighbor opened it. He was about to have dinner, when he heard the knock on the door.

"Hello Sandra," he said. "What's the matter?"

Sandra was visibly very worried. "Have you seen anybody suspicious outside our house? Isabelle is missing. She was in the crib sleeping! When Thomas got home, she was missing! I was cooking in the kitchen."

The neighbor sees that she is concerned. "Oh dear!" he said. "I haven't seen anybody, but I'll help you search for her."

The neighbor informed other nearby neighbors about the situation. They all came out and started searching around.

A couple minutes later, the police arrived. There were two police officers and a dog. Thomas went over and spoke to them.

"Officer, somebody kidnapped our baby. The window in the bedroom was opened."

"We'll investigate further," said one of the officers. "Please stay calm."

The other police officer got the dog out of the car and headed towards the house. The police entered the house, while neighbors were searching outside.

The police first started searching the bedroom and looking for evidence. They saw the window opened but found nothing else. The neighbors, meanwhile, were in the backyard and in the gardens with their flashlights. The police continued searching the rest of the house. After a few minutes of searching, the police found nothing. They then went outside and started searching with the neighbors.

In a tall tree across the street near the farm, Bigfoot was watching them.

During the search, the police noticed a suspicious-looking garbage can upside down in the backyard. They looked beneath it and found Isabelle there on the grass. The police looked stunned.

"We found her, Mr. and Mrs. Duncan," he said. "She was under this garbage can."

"Oh my God," said Sandra. "Our baby! Thank you so much, officer!"

Thomas was confused and skeptical about the situation.

"Something doesn't appear right, though," he said. "She doesn't appear to have any type of reaction."

The first neighbor Sandra approached came over to them.

"I'm glad you found her, but I have to go now."

As other neighbors started leaving as well, Sandra said, "Thank you all for helping us!"

"Yes," said Thomas, "thank you!"

The police pulled them aside. "If you think there's something wrong with her," one officer said, "we'll help you get to the hospital."

"Thank you, officer," said Thomas. "Maybe that would be a good idea."

And so, the police took the Duncans to the hospital.

When they arrived, the police dropped them off, and Thomas and Sandra brought Isabelle inside. They talked to the person at the front desk and then waited in the lobby. They got called in by a nurse. Thirty minutes later, Thomas and Sandra were waiting for the doctor's verdict outside in the hall. Then, the doctor called them in.

"Based on the lab results, there appears to be nothing wrong with her, she's healthy."

Sandra is confused. "Are you sure, doctor?"

The doctor nods. "We have checked everything we could check, she is perfectly fine. If there is something wrong, we would notice."

They left the hospital and went outside to call for a cab, Thomas looked at his wife and saw that she was worried.

Thomas tried to relax her. "Don't worry, honey. The doctor said she is fine."

Sandra calmed down a bit. "Alright, alright."

"Thankfully Thomas and Sandra have put that event in the past," said Mara, "but I have a feeling that Isabelle is still not right. When I was with her before the kidnapping, she was very energetic and was so interested in everything around her. But now, she seems so lethargic."

Kayla started getting a bit worried for Alice. "I hope that doesn't happen to Alice."

"I hope so, too," said Mara.

Chapter III

Unwanted Ingredient

It was 7 PM at Crowded Lake, and Alice's family had just finished dinner. Alex, Ronald, Kayla, Mara, and Alice were all there. Mara was putting leftover food away. It consisted of sliced-up banana bread and fried chicken. She put the banana bread on a shelf and the fried chicken in the oven. Kayla went to the living room to watch TV.

"Hey everyone," Kayla said, "there's a great TV show playing right now."

Ronald came in the room too. "Let's watch it."

Meanwhile, Alex was playing with his toys in his room. Alice entered the living room and started watching TV with her parents. Kayla called out to Mara.

"Mom, what are you doing? Come here and watch the show with us!"

"I'm putting the leftover food away," Mara called back. "I can't right now."

Around thirty minutes later, Alice got ready to go to sleep. Kayla was in the room with her, helping Alice get ready for bed. Kayla then sat down and read a short story to Alice. After that, Kayla gave her a goodnight kiss and got ready to turn off the lights.

"Good night, sweetie. See you tomorrow in the morning."

"Good night, Mom. I love you."

"I love you, too."

Kayla turned off the lights and exited the room. In the living room, Ronald was asleep on the couch. When Kayla saw that Ronald had fallen asleep, she turned off the TV and went to check on Alex. In Alex's room, Alex had already gone to sleep. She put a blanket over him, turned off the lights, and slowly exited the room. Mara was already asleep in her room, too.

A few hours later, Bigfoot entered the kitchen through the backdoor. Everybody had already gone to sleep. Bigfoot went to some of the leftover banana bread on a shelf. He opened the shelf and took the bread out. The kitchen was dark. A few minutes later, Bigfoot put the bread back on the shelf and exited the house through the backdoor.

A few more hours after that, Kayla heard something downstairs. She woke up and went out to the hall. She went to the stairway and saw Mara in the kitchen. Mara greeted her.

"Oh, hello, Kayla! Good morning. How was your sleep?"

"It was great," Kayla said. "What are you doing here so early?"

"I'm going to make breakfast for you all," she said and took out a bowl.

"What are you going to cook?" Kayla asked.

"Banana bread pudding."

Mara started cracking eggs and putting them into the bowl.

"Sounds delicious!" Kayla said.

Alex came down to the kitchen.

"Hey big guy," Kayla said cheerfully. "Good morning! How are you doing?"

"Good morning, Mom. I'm doing well."

"Guess what? Grandma is cooking banana bread pudding, your favorite!"

Ronald came in, staggering, yawning, and covering his mouth.

"Good morning. How is everybody doing?" he asked.

"Everybody is doing fine!" said Kayla, "Right, everybody? How are you doing?"

Ronald drowsily said, "I'm just tired."

"Well, breakfast is coming," said Kayla.

Mara went to retrieve some leftover banana bread from the shelf because she was ready to make the banana bread pudding. She took out the bread and saw that the food has turned dark brown. She was confused and started thinking on what's gone on with the bread. Then, she noticed a terrible smell coming from it. Knowing what it was, Mara got angry and went out into the backyard.

Everybody was confused and looked at each other. Ronald was bewildered.

"What happened? What's going on?"

Kayla, said, "I don't know!"

Out in the backyard, Mara was shouting at a tall cherry tree in the backyard.

"Bigfoot, you piece of crap! You pissed on my food! Where are you!?! Come out, let me piss on your face and see how you like it! Come on, hideous freak! Come out and show yourself! Don't just come out when nobody is around! I know you hear me, damn you!"

Everybody rushed to the backyard.

Meanwhile, Alice was just coming down the stairs.

"Mommy, mommy! Mommy? Where are you?"

"What's going on, Grandma?" asked Alex.

Mara was furious. "Bigfoot pissed on the food that I saved for today!"

"Oh, that's terrible!" said Alex.

Alice heard the commotion at the backyard door and was curious on what was going on.

"Mom! What's happening?"

"Nothing, sweetie. Come on let's go back to the kitchen," Kayla said and brought her back inside.

Mara re-entered the kitchen with Alex and Ronald following her and went over to the leftover food on the shelf.

"Yuck!" said Ronald. "What's that smell?"

Alex covered his nose. "That's disgusting!"

Kayla said, "It smells bad, and it looks disgusting. We're just gonna have to throw it away, Mom."

Alice saw the leftover food and was curious. "What is that? Let me see, let me see!"

As she approaches the food, she smelled it. "Ew, what's that smell?"

"Bigfoot piss," said Alex in a comedic tone.

Alice said, "Yuck!"

However, Mara was still upset. "Damn, Bigfoot!" she said to herself.

"Kayla is right," said Mara to the rest of the family. "We have to throw away the food. Sorry, everyone. I'll cook scrambled eggs and pancakes, instead. No banana bread pudding for this morning."

"That's really odd," said Ronald. "How do you know it's Bigfoot?"

"Well, it has that very awful smell, and it's a very dark shade of brown."

"It smells like clothes that haven't been worn or washed and buried in a closet for a long time," Kayla said.

"Oh, yeah!" Ronald agreed.

"That's exactly what Bigfoot smells like!" said Mara. "Before Kayla got married to you, I saw a big, tall, and hairy creature leaving this house through the back door, and it climbed up in that big, tall tree over there." She pointed to the tall cherry tree. "And besides, who would piss on our food?"

"Fair point," said Ronald. "I understand now."

Chapter IV
Early Arrival

On the outskirts of Crowded Lake, there were some friends of the Adkins family—Alfie Scott and his wife Audrey. The outskirts of Crowded Lake consisted of many more bushes than normal and were much closer to the farms. The houses, including Alfie's and Audrey's house, were surrounded by bushes and tall trees and were much more spread apart. This region of Crowded Lake was farther from the cities, and the nearest city would be around seventeen miles away.

One evening in early September, Alfie and Audrey were invited to a party. They were very excited. They were dressed up and ready to go.

"Are you ready, honey?" Alfie asked.

"Five minutes!"

"Okay, I'll be waiting in the living room."

Soon, Audrey came out and they walked towards their friend's house. It was not that far, it was only a block away.

When they reached the front door, they could hear music from inside. The house was filled with people. Alfie knocked on the door as loud as he could, and his friend opened the door. The friend was named Anderson.

"Hey Alfie, hey Audrey! Welcome to my party. I'm glad you could come!"

"Thanks for having us," Alfie said.

Audrey cheerfully said, "Yes, thank you!"

"No problem!" said Anderson and walked them over to over to the living room. "Have fun and enjoy!"

"Sure, thank you!" said Audrey.

The people at the party were having fun, dancing, drinking, and eating. They were also playing party games and watching movies.

A few hours later, Audrey was getting sleepy and wanted to go home and get some rest. Alfie didn't want to go, yet. Audrey called Anderson over.

"Hey Anderson, I'm tired. I have to go, unfortunately."

"Aww that's too bad, can't you stay a little longer?"

"I can't," said Audrey. "I'm too tired. I had a lot of work to do, today. I also have to get up early, tomorrow. Alfie can stay here, though."

"I'll walk you home and come back to the party," said Alfie.

Anderson said, "Okay, bye Audrey!"

Then Alfie walked Audrey back home.

When they arrive, he said, "Alright Audrey, I'll come back home in the morning. See you soon."

"Okay, bye," said Audrey.

Inside she went to her room, got in her night gown, turned off the lights, and went to bed.

A few hours later, while she was half-asleep, the front door opened. However, Audrey ignored it, thinking it was her husband. She went back to sleep. She noticed a terrible smell when he got into bed. She ignored that too, thinking it was just a leftover odor her husband got from the party. She was also too sleepy to care, and she didn't think that it was anybody else, anyway. Nevertheless, about one hour later, she felt him get up—her husband getting up early for some reason—but she was still sleepy.

With her eyes closed and in a sleepy tone, she asked, "Where are you going? Why are you getting up so early?"

There was a grunt in reply.

Then, she heard the front door opening. This time, it was Alfie who entered.

"Hello?" he called from downstairs. "Audrey?"

Wondering who she'd been sleeping with, she hastily turned around.

To her surprise, Bigfoot has started leaving. Bigfoot was around seven feet tall with broad shoulders and covered in hair all over his body. He had a strong odor, smelling like dirty clothes that have been buried in a closet for a couple years. Audrey couldn't see him well, however; it was too dark in the room.

Alfie started walking towards her room and saw Bigfoot walking away. He was also in shock. Bigfoot walked towards the back door, went out into the backyard, and disappeared into the bushes. Bigfoot never said anything.

"I thought that was you!" Audrey said. "I thought you came home early. I didn't know that was Bigfoot in the bed with me!"

Alfie rushed through the backdoor after Bigfoot, but the creature had already disappeared. Alfie starts screaming towards the bushes.

"Bigfoot, you hairy, smelly scoundrel! You sleep with my wife!? Get your own wife, you filthy animal! You are a sneaky coward!"

Audrey said, "Call the police!"

"What for?" Alfie said. "That stinky reprobate has already disappeared into the woods. They can't really do anything about it now."

At noon later that day, Audrey went to a nearby convenience store. She saw her friend and neighbor, Kayla Adkins, coming out from the store.

"Hey Kayla!" she said. "How are you doing? What you got there?"

"I'm doing fine. I just got some groceries. How are you doing?"

"I'm also doing fine," Audrey said. "Thank you for asking."

"Hey, did you go to Anderson's party, last night?" Kayla asked. "I got invited, but I couldn't come. My mother was sick, and my husband had to go to the city, so he came back late."

"Yeah, but I didn't stay for long. My husband stayed until four, though. I had problems last night. When Alfie was still at the party, Bigfoot entered the house and got in my bed. I thought it was Alfie, so I didn't say anything. But around an hour later, Alfie got home. Then, I wondered who was with me, and it turned out to be Bigfoot. The weirdest part was how Bigfoot just calmly walked away into the bushes outside and just vanished! Alfie tried to go after him, but Bigfoot was already gone. I didn't really believe Bigfoot, until last night."

Kayla responded with wonder. "I haven't seen Bigfoot, but my mother did. I have only encountered what Bigfoot can do, which is piss on leftover food during the night when everybody is asleep. Bigfoot seems to like playing tricks on people. That sounds very strange, but it's possible. It happened to my family, too. My mother saw Bigfoot inside the house before, when I was still single."

Audrey said, "How odd!"

"Audrey, I got to run home. Talk to you later, bye!"

"Bye Kayla, have a great day!"

"You too!"

Chapter V

Reveals & Fireflies

It had been six years since Isabelle Duncan was abducted. Isabelle was now six years old. Alice was now seven. It was around 3 PM, and Thomas Duncan was speaking to the teacher on the phone about Isabelle.

"Sir, your daughter is struggling in school, and we're worried that she might not be able to succeed in the future."

"How can that be?" Thomas said.

"I'm not sure. She might require special help to get her back on track."

"Okay," said Thomas. "Thank you for letting me know."

Thomas hung up the phone and went to Sandra.

"A teacher told me that Isabelle isn't doing well in school," he said.

Sandra wondered what was going on. "Is she being bad in school? Not behaving?"

"No, she just can't get good grades. The teacher said we should get like a tutor or something."

Sandra grew sad and Thomas noticed this.

"Don't worry, I will do whatever I have to do to make sure Isabelle succeeds."

A few hours later, at the Adkins' house, Mara was watching TV. Alex, now eleven, was in his room, on the computer. Ronald and Kayla were outside on the lawn looking at the full moon. Alice was with them, counting the stars. Kayla had spoken on phone before to Sandra, so she knew what was going on with Isabelle.

"Sandra asked me if I knew a good tutor," she said.

"Why is that?" Ronald asked.

"Isabelle is not doing well in school. Do you think it has something to do with Bigfoot?"

Ronald (not knowing that Bigfoot is around) said, "It's possible, but it could be reasonably explained. Some people just need extra help."

"Probably," said Kayla, "because Alice was abducted by Bigfoot, too. She's fine, though."

Alice heard her parents talking and jumped in the conversation.

"Mom, I was not abducted by Bigfoot."

Kayla was surprised. "What?! What do you mean?"

"Yes," said Ronald, "What do you mean, Alice? Two years ago, you told us that you were."

Which is when Alice described what actually happened that night.

Two years ago, Alice had been sitting near the bushes on a bench in a park, when a neighbor from across the street—Jane Bates—walked towards her. Jane mostly lived alone, across the street from the playground.

"Hey Alice, how are you doing? Why are you sitting here alone?"

Alice knew Jane well. She was a soft-spoken woman in her late twenties.

"I'm tired," Alice said. "I'm taking a break."

"Would you like to see my new kitten? It's very cute."

"Oh sure," said Alice. "Where is it?"

"It's in my house, want to come?"

"Okay."

And so Alice followed Jane to her house.

Her house was small, surrounded by bushes, and had dogwood trees in front of the property. When they arrive, Jane points to her cat.

"Here he is!" she said.

"Oh, he's so cute!" Alice said.

"Yeah, isn't he adorable?"

"What's his name?"

Jane thought for a second. "I'm still figuring out a name. What do you think?"

"What about Kitty?"

"Kitty sounds nice," said Jane. "Let's go with that!"

Alice started petting the kitten. "Here Kitty Kitty!"

"Sweetheart, are you hungry?" said Alice. "Would you like a banana and some milk?"

"Sure!"

So Jane got her a banana and a glass of milk.

Then Jane heard a commotion outside. She locked the door and heard Alice's parents looking for her. Jane got worried.

"Alice, your parents are looking for you," Jane said.

"But I want to sleep here with the kitten!" said Alice.

"Your parents will be very worried if they don't see you." Jane was also worried about her own safety, afraid that Alice's parents would find out. And so Jane thought up a plan.

"You can play with Kitty for a while longer. Then when nobody is around, go to your home. Tell your parents that you were abducted by Bigfoot. Can you do that?"

"Okay," Alice said. "That's like the creature from the stories grandma tells me."

A little while later, Jane unlocked the door and looked outside. She saw nobody around.

"Okay Alice, go and stay safe, sweetie! I will watch you from here."

Jane gave Alice a kiss goodbye. Alice started walking towards her house.

When Alice was finished telling the real version of events, Kayla was a little stunned.

"Alice, just go play with your friends over at the park. Make sure not to stay out too late and not to go too far. Just stay nearby and come home soon."

"Okay, Mom, I will."

Alice went to play with her friends, leaving Ronald and Kayla standing on the lawn, shocked.

"Do you believe that?" Kayla said.

"Yeah, I believe her in a way."

"Should we do something about Jane?" she asked.

"Nah, I know Jane Bates. She has good intentions. Besides, she's already moved."

Before long they went back in the house.

Alice was sitting on the swing when she saw a firefly. Then another and another. Her close friends Benjamin Patel and Owen Todd started chasing after the fireflies. Benjamin, Owen, and Alice were close friends and neighbors. Alice followed them.

"They're getting away!" Benjamin said.

"Most of them are heading along the street!" said Owen. "Let's get them!"

Alice kept following them. They soon crossed a bridge over the river and got to the other side. They were now at the area of the neighborhood where there were lots of bushes and trees. Benjamin and Owen were near the bushes, trying to catch the fireflies. Benjamin managed to swat a firefly out of the air.

"I got one, I got one!" he said as the firefly fell onto the ground.

All of a sudden, Owen started running away. Benjamin ran away soon after. Alice, not knowing what's going on, tried to pick up the firefly. She was near some bushes. There was a rustling noises behind the bushes. When she turned around, she saw something moving in the bushes. Something threw gravel at her. She started running as fast as she could to the park.

Benjamin and Owen were waiting.

"Hey! You ran away without me! I got rocks thrown on me!"

"Haven't you heard, yet?" said Owen. "Somebody saw Bigfoot in those bushes! That's why I ran!"

Benjamin said, "You must've confronted Bigfoot!"

"Oh, I didn't know!"

But Alice was scared because nobody was outside, and it was almost nighttime.

"It's late," said Benjamin. "We should go home."

After they had all said their goodbyes and headed home, Alice wondered if she should tell her parents about what happened. She was worried that her parents wouldn't believe her or that she might get in trouble for not listening to them and going far away from the area.

Chapter VI

Visiting a Sick Relative

It was fall of 2014, and Ronald was sitting in the living room one day coming up to 5 PM. The phone started to ring, and after a couple of rings, he picked up.

"Hello, who is this?"

"*It's Debra.*"

Ronald was taken by surprise.

"Oh, how are you doing? What's going on?"

Debra was his sister-in-law, his brother Adam's wife.

"*It's not going well over here, Adam is really sick. Would you come visit him?*"

"Sure, I'll bring Kayla with me."

"*Okay, thank you. I'll see you in a bit.*"

Ronald found Kayla in the laundry room. "Hey Kayla, we have to go visit Adam. He's sick."

"That's terrible," she said. "Give me a few minutes and we can go."

Kayla called for Alice who was watching TV in the living room.

When she came over, Kayla asked, "Alice, where is your grandmother?"

"She's in the garden, picking up some vegetables."

"Why don't you help her?" Kayla asked.

"She didn't want me to help."

"And where's your brother?"

"He's at his friend's house," Alice said, noticing that her mother was getting ready to go somewhere. "Where are you going?"

"Your Uncle Adam is really sick."

"Can I come?" Alice asked. "I want to visit him, too."

"No," said Kayla, "you just stay right here."

"Please, please, Mom?"

"Just let her come," said Ronald.

"Alright," Kayla said, "get dressed. Let's go."

Kayla found Mara in the garden. "Mother, we have to go. Ronald's brother Adam is really sick."

"Okay, dear," Said Mara. "I'll see you later. Tell Adam that I wish him well."

"I will."

Ronald, Kayla, and Alice walked the three blocks to Ronald's brother's house. When they arrived, Ronald knocked on the door. The house, on the outside, was very messy. The grass was not cut, trash was laying outside on the side, and some of the paint on the house was peeling away. The house itself was old and big. Debra opened the door and greeted them. She looked exhausted, and her hair was messy.

"Hey," she said, "I'm glad you guys were able to come! Hey Alice, you're looking great today!"

"Hey Auntie, thank you!"

Debra gave Alice a hug.

"Hello Kayla," she said. "How are you?"

"I'm doing well, how about you?"

"I'm a bit tired, but I'm just worried for Adam."

Kayla gives her a hug. "It's going to be fine," she said. "We're here to help out."

They entered the house and found that, like the outside, it was messy and dirty inside. It was out of sync with the rest of the neighborhood. The dishes weren't washed, the walls weren't fully painted, and the floor was dirty.

"I'm sorry the house is messy," said Debra, picking up some things on the floor. "I didn't have time to clean up the house."

"I can help clean," said Kayla.

"Oh thank you!"

They saw Adam lying in bed.

"Hey," said Ronald politely, "how are you feeling?"

"I'm not feeling so well."

"Did you go to the doctor?"

"Yes, I just got back from the hospital a couple hours ago. I got some medicine. I think it's time to take it again."

"Here," said Ronald, "let me help you." Ronald then proceeded to help his brother with the medicine.

Adam then turned to his other visitors. "Hey Kayla and Alice, how are you?"

"We're doing fine," Kayla said. "My mother wishes you well."

"Oh, tell her I said thank you."

"How's school, Alice?" asked Debra.

"It's going well, Auntie."

"I'm glad to hear that." She then turned to Kayla. "Can I get you anything to eat or drink?"

"No, Debra, I am fine for now."

"How about you, Ronald?"

"I'll just have a glass of water."

Debra then turned to Alice. "Alice, how about you?"

"I'm fine, Auntie. Thank you."

Debra went to the kitchen to bring Ronald a glass of water.

About an hour later, it was almost dinner time. Debra was trying to clean the kitchen so she could cook something.

"Debra," said Ronald, "let's just order food instead. You don't have to cook."

"Are you sure, Ronald? I can cook if needed."

"Yes, I'm sure. Just get some rest."

"Okay, then."

Ronald turned to his daughter. "Alice, you have to go home to get up early for school."

"Can we eat dinner first?"

"Your grandmother is going to be cooking dinner, so it's fine. You have dinner at home."

"Okay. Bye Auntie, I got to go home."

"Alright dear, just be careful out there!" she said and gave Alice a hug again.

"Bye, Alice!"

As she went to leave, Ronald said, "Stay safe, Alice! Just go straight home!"

A few minutes later, Alice was walking towards her house, which was around one block away. Nobody was around, and it was getting dark. To the right, there was a house with a dimmed light in front of it. When she was passing by that house, there was gravel thrown at her from a tall tree in front of it, surrounded by bushes.

Alice started running as fast as she could until she reached home.

When she got home, Mara was there. She knocked on the door. When Mara opened the door, Alice was exhausted from running.

"Are you alright, dear?" her grandmother asked. "Where is your mom and dad?"

"I'm okay, grandma. They have to stay at Uncle Adam's house, because Auntie is by herself and Uncle Adam is really, really sick. Where's Alex?"

"He's having dinner in the kitchen," Mara said. "Are you hungry? Go join him."

"Okay, grandma."

Ronald and Kayla were tired. They could not sleep at Adam's home, so they decided to go home.

"Hey Debra, we have to head back. Adam is asleep now, I hope he gets better by tomorrow. Call me if anything happens."

"Okay, Ronald. Thank you so much for visiting us, I really appreciate it."

"It's no problem," Kayla said. "It was our pleasure."

"The least I can do for my brother," said Ronald.

Ronald and Kayla exited the house and started walking home. They were passing the same area where Alice got gravel thrown at her, and as they approach the dim-lit house with the large tree and bushes on the right, Kayla saw someone going to the house across from it. The house across from it belonged to Kayla's Uncle James, and she thought it was her uncle covered in a blanket.

But it wasn't. It was Bigfoot.

As the figure was walking away, Kayla called to him. "James? Is that you?"

Bigfoot responded with a grunt then walked towards a tall plum tree in front of her uncle's house, climbed it, then vanished.

Kayla was shocked and scared, and started to hold Ronald's arm tight.

"Ronald, did you see that?!"

"What? What happened?"

"You didn't see that?"

"What happened, what did you see?"

"It was Bigfoot! I thought it was my uncle in a blanket, but he went up that tall tree and disappeared!"

Ronald stayed calm and kept walking home. He understood what had happened and was not afraid. Kayla continued to hold his arm tight and never looked back until they reached the house.

Chapter VII

"Someone must have been very hungry."

In summer of 2015 Alice was twelve, and Alex was sixteen. It was around one in the afternoon, and Mara was cleaning up the house while Kayla washed dishes. Ronald, Alex, and Alice were getting ready to leave and go to the garden.

"Kayla, we're leaving to the garden," Ronald said.

"When you guys get home," Kayla said, "supper will be ready."

"Sounds good, let's go guys."

"Be careful out there," Mara said. "Watch out for Bigfoot!"

"Alright, grandma!" said Alice.

And Alex said, "Okay, grandma."

But Ronald said, "Come on Mara, there is no such as Bigfoot in the daytime."

Ronald was carrying a chainsaw, Alex an axe, and Alice a machete as they walked to the red pickup truck. The garden was secluded and only two blocks away. However, they were going to be chopping and gathering wood. The garden featured some fruit trees: apple, pears, cherries, and was surrounded by tall native trees and bushes. There were other gardens nearby that connect to a giant farm.

When they reached the garden, Alex noticed a smell coming from the garden.

"I smell somebody cooking."

Ronald looked around. "Maybe it's one of the neighbors," he said and pointed to a house.

"Or maybe Bigfoot," said Alice.

"Nah," said Alex, "it can't be."

They entered the garden and saw smoke from a fire. The fire was nearby some trees and bushes. They saw broken apple boughs lying around the fire.

"It looks like somebody vandalized our garden," said Ronald.

Alex was surprised. "We were robbed?"

"It looks like it. Now I wonder who would have done such a thing."

"Somebody must have been very hungry," said Alice.

Then, Alex turned his eyes towards some tall trees and bushes near the farm. He caught a glimpse of a big creature with hair walking towards the farm. Alex tried to chase it, but it disappeared.

Alice ran after him. "What is it, Alex?"

Ronald asked, "Did you see anything?"

"I thought I saw something big, but when I went after it, it vanished."

"See," said Alice. "I told you it must have been Bigfoot. There's nobody around here, nobody even in the farm."

"Let's just start cutting some wood," Ronald said.

An hour and a half later, they had started cutting the branches of a tree Ronald had felled, but Alice wanted to go to her cousin's house nearby.

"Dad, I'm tired, I want to go to Lucy's."

"Alright," said Ronald, "just don't go anywhere else."

Her cousin's house was only a block away from her house. Lucy and Alice were very close. They were around the same age and attended the same school. They liked to hang out with each other occasionally. Alice left the garden.

At around 4 PM, Alex and Ronald arrived. Kayla was in front of the house.

"Where's Alice?"

"She's with Lucy," he said and opened the tailgate of the pickup truck filled with wood.

"You know Alice," Alex said, "Whenever she's off school, she never wants to stay home."

"So she's at Lucy's house?"

"That's where she said she was going," said Ronald.

"I'm starving!" said Alex.

"Your grandma cooked supper," said Kayla. "go to the kitchen, and get something to eat! Your grandma is in there."

After Alex went inside, Kayla said, "Alice and Lucy, those two are like sisters."

Kayla started getting wood from the truck and carrying it to the backyard. "At least we know where she's at."

At Lucy's house, Alice was saying goodbye to her cousin.

"I have to go. My mother must be waiting for me. Bye Lucy!"

"Bye Alice, see you tomorrow!"

"You don't want to sleep over?" Lucy's mom asked.

"No, Auntie, I have to go home."

"Alright then, stay safe."

Alice gives Lucy and her mother a hug and left. A few minutes later, she passed near a garden with some bushes and tall trees. Suddenly, gravel was thrown right at her. Alice started running as fast as she could to her house.

The next day, Alice came to Lucy's House and knocked on the door. Her bike was left nearby on the street.

"Hey Lucy! Are you there?"

Alice knocked again, and Lucy's mother opened the door.

"Oh, Lucy! Alice is here!"

When Lucy came out Alice said, "Hey, let's go!"

"Where's your bike?"

Alice points at her bike. "Right over there."

Lucy went back inside to get her own bike. Before they left, Lucy's mother spoke to them.

"Stay safe, you two! Don't go too far, and don't come home too late!"

"Okay, Mom," said Lucy.

Alice said, "We will, Auntie."

As they were walking towards Alice's bike, she said, "Hey Lucy, yesterday I passed by these large bushes and trees. Suddenly, a bunch of gravel got thrown at me. I think it was Bigfoot!"

"Really?" said Lucy, "I have heard about people talking about Bigfoot, but I was always skeptical about it."

They then got on their bikes and rode away.

Fifteen minutes later, they got near the river. Lucy was riding fast, and Alice was farther behind her. Alice called to her.

"Hey Lucy, wait up!"

Lucy looked back and stopped near some shade. Alice approached and stopped nearby. They were tired.

Lucy said, "Let's take a break."

They stopped nearby a garden on the opposite side of the river.

Then, Lucy smelled something. "Hey Alice, do you smell something? I smell somebody cooking from the garden. I don't see anybody around, though."

Alice was curious. "Let's go check it out."

Lucy has a different idea. "Let's just get going."

"Come on," said Alice. "It's daytime. Maybe somebody is cooking something."

They started approaching the area. Then they saw a fire. Nobody was around. They saw tree stumps rooted out of the ground and leaves on the ground.

Lucy was confused, but Alice knew who it was.

Alice quickly said, "Nobody is around, let's go."

They got back on their bikes and rode away. However, Bigfoot was watching them from the bushes as they were walking away to their bikes.

Chapter VIII

Destruction & Relocation

In the summer of 2017, Alice was fourteen, and Alex was eighteen. Alice was outside of the neighborhood, since her school was about fifteen miles from Crowded Lake. She was riding her bike. Benjamin and Owen were with her because they were going to the same school. Meanwhile, Alex was at a morning high school, also about fifteen miles away. Ronald was at his job near by the city. Kayla and Mara were cooking at home.

When Alice was halfway to school when she saw something flying in the sky. There was a tornado heading straight for the neighborhood. Alice stopped and watched in awe.

Benjamin said, "Hey, maybe we should go back home. It looks like there is a tornado."

Alice remained calm. "I don't think so, I didn't hear anything about a tornado." Alice continued to ride her bike to school.

"Yeah," said Owen, "let's just continue heading towards school."

When they reached school, some people were discussing about the tornado.

"It looks like there is a terrible storm outside," a teacher said.

Alice and Owen approached. "Is there actually a tornado?" Owen asked. "Is it going to hit Crowded Lake?"

Another teacher said, "According to the news, it already went past a small town. There are seven wounded. Some houses were wiped out. We might have to cancel school."

"Oh, that's terrible!" said Alice. "I hope those seven people are okay."

Alice, Benjamin, and Owen quickly rushed back to Crowded Lake. Before they entered the neighborhood, they saw trees and powerlines on the street. They couldn't enter yet.

At Crowded Lake, police, firefighters, and paramedics were there to keep the area safe and to help people who had suffered from the damage. There were volunteers working to clear up the streets. They were all shocked.

"Oh my God," said Benjamin, worried, "I hope my family is okay. This is quite the disaster."

"Me, too," said Alice.

Owen said, "Let's get home to see what happened."

A couple minutes later, they reached their homes. Benjamin dropped his bike in front of the house and ran inside. He later found out that his family was fine. However, the house suffered minor damage.

When Owen arrived at his home, his mother told him that that his father was injured while outside during the storm. The house also suffered minor damage. They had to rush him to the hospital later that day.

When Alice got home, she saw that most of the roof had been destroyed, and the front door had flown from its hinges. Mara was holding her hand.

"What happened, Grandma?"

Mara tried to stay calm. "I was trying to keep the front door shut, but the wind blew the door right off and hit my hand."

Oh, I'm so sorry to hear that, Grandma," said Alice. "Where's Mom?"

"She's in the kitchen, she's fine. She was holding the window, but the window, thankfully, didn't blow away."

"Do you need to go to the hospital, Grandma?"

"No, dear, I will be fine."

"Are you sure, Grandma?"

"Yes, dear, I'm sure."

Just then Alex arrived home. "I heard that there was a tornado, so I came home early. Where's Dad?"

Mara said, "He's still at work."

Alice went to the kitchen. "Mom, are you okay?"

"I'm fine, sweetie. How about you?"

"I wasn't here, I was going to school. I saw a bunch of debris flying in the sky. I wasn't sure if it was a tornado or not."

Ronald arrived, panic-stricken, "Is everybody okay? I heard and saw what happened."

"Oh, thank God, you are home! Look at this mess."

"It's not as bad as the middle of the neighborhood," Ronald said. "The tornado hit that area the hardest, and most the houses were wiped out. Some people lost everything."

"Oh, that's terrible!" said Kayla.

Ronald said, "I saw many volunteers helping out and donation booths nearby the neighborhood, though. I think the neighborhood will recover soon."

In Crowded Lake, the middle part of the neighborhood was, indeed, the area most affected by the tornado. The tornado had torn through the large area of Crowded Lake, while the smaller areas didn't suffer as much damage. Volunteers and paramedics were still helping the victims and clearing the roads. Ronald, Kayla, Mara, Alex, and Alice started cleaning up the house and tidying up. Ronald and Alex tried fixing the roof. Kayla tried to replace the front door. Alice helped clean up some of the mess, and Mara helped some relatives, who were staying at their house, to get comfortable.

The next day, Alex and Ronald went out to help out the rest of the neighborhood. Most of the neighborhood had been cleared, and houses were being rebuilt. Alex and Ronald were with other volunteers to help clear out the rest of the roads. Some volunteers had decided to cut down some tall trees and bushes because of possible urbanization. They decided to repair the roads and build more houses with bricks and other strong materials instead of just wood, so that the houses would be more secure.

The other side of the neighborhood was more affected by this, since it had lots of shrubbery and too many tall trees. It was also the older part of the neighborhood, which had many more wooden houses.

Nearby in a tree surrounded by bushes, Bigfoot watched as volunteers cut down the trees and bushes. Later, Bigfoot moved away to a denser and more secluded area. It is unknown if anybody will ever see Bigfoot in that general area again.

Afterword

These stories are actually based on true stories, with some of main characters being based off my mother's family, her relatives, and her close neighbors. In fact, the name Crowded Lake is a translated version of the real name of her town in Indonesia called *Tlogorejo*. Crowded Lake is a fictionalized version of Tlogorejo set in Washington state.

The real town, like Crowded Lake, is far away from cities. It has many gardens where people plant tapioca trees, sweet potatoes, bananas, citrus fruit, plum trees, coconuts, and many other types of shrubbery. These gardens are surrounded by tall trees and bushes. Houses are usually not close to each other and are separated by some distance. Everybody in the neighborhood knows each other.

The real-life girl Isabelle was based on never actually finished school and currently lives with her mother in Java. She is married to a man who is around twenty years older than her. She has one son. The person Alice was based on first came to the United States in 2000. The person Lucy was based on was just a friendly neighbor.

Some stories, such as the rock throwing, were combined with other stories that were completely separate. Some major differences between this story and what actually happened in Indonesia are the following:

This all happened in the late twentieth century, from around the early 1970s to the early 1980s. Tlogorejo is also quite different from Crowded Lake; it was more of a rural village with no electricity and no phones. Only a few people had TVs. Police were stationed about an hour away. Instead, two people took turns every night to guard the village. There was only one elementary school, and that was the only kind of school in the area. The closest high school was thirty minutes away when driving. There were mango trees, tapioca trees, plum trees, and cherry trees. There was actually no lake in Tlogorejo, despite the name meaning roughly Crowded Lake. Instead, there was simply a river and a small creek in the village. Cars were very rare to see in the area.

Bigfoot was referred to as *Gendruwo*. Gendruwo and Bigfoot are usually the same, when it comes to what people normally think of Bigfoot. All the chapters are altered and changed from what actually happened. For example, in Chapter VII, during the woodcutting, the person representing Ronald is the one who actually saw Gendruwo instead of the person representing Alex. In fact, in real life he saw Gendruwo several times in the same area. He saw Gendruwo hanging in a tree at the corner of the garden and saw Gendruwo behind a tree towards the farm.

In the actual story "Alice" and "Lucy" are supposed to actually be collecting wood nearby a neighbor's garden instead of riding bikes together. When Alice had rocks thrown on her for a third time, she was actually coming home from watching TV in a neighbor's house.

This story was originally a TV script that I wrote for a script challenge for a reward in a cash. That is what inspired me to actually make this into a book. I first heard these stories from my mother who started telling them to me when I was five years old. Thank you for reading this story. If you enjoyed it, it would be greatly appreciated if you share it with close friends and family. I personally think that this is a story that people would enjoy to read and listen to.

www.ingramcontent.com/pod-product-compliance
Lightning Source LLC
LaVergne TN
LVHW011859060526
838200LV00054B/4425